Eugene MAGALIF

For Tanya
for Flute and Piano
(with optional Flute 2 and Wind Chimes)

For my lovely wife

Full Score

For my lovely wife

For TANYA

Eugene Magalif, ASCAP

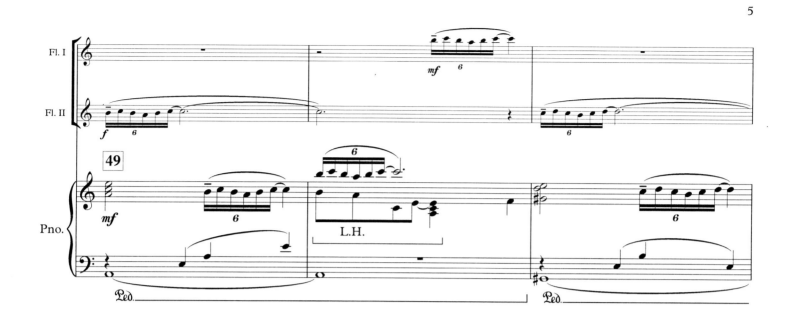

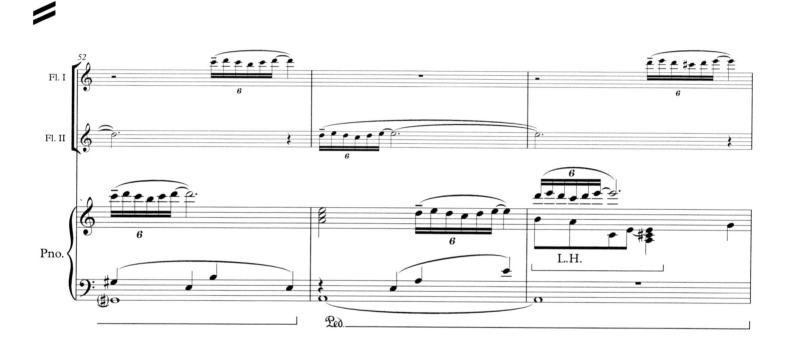

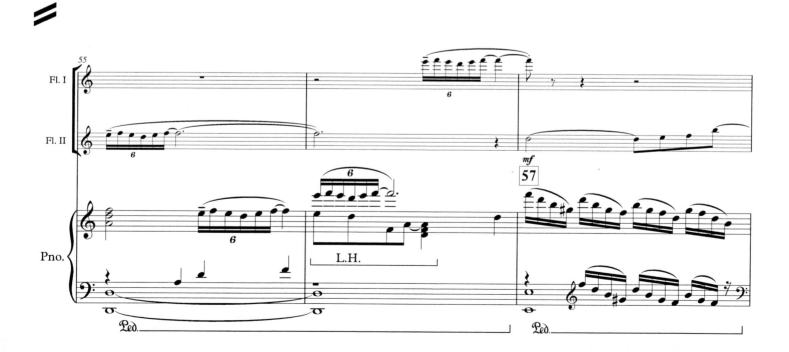

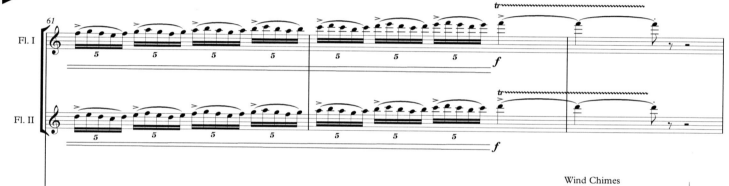

4

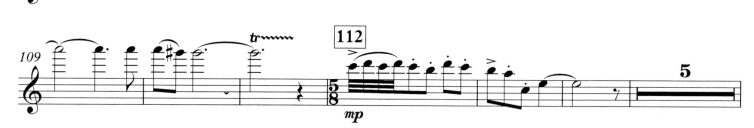

Flute I

For my lovely wife
For TANYA

Eugene Magalif, ASCAP

SU810

Eugene MAGALIF

For Tanya
for Flute and Piano
(with optional Flute 2 and Wind Chimes)

For my lovely wife

rit. _

Adagio ♩ = 76

5'53.0"

SOUTHERN MUSIC FLUTE WORKS
SELECTED FLUTE EDITIONS/ ARRANGEMENTS

COLLECTIONS

Nancy Andrews
Paris Conservatory Album: 16 Short Lyric Pieces — B579 - HL240976
Gilbert and Sullivan, arr. Galway/ Overton
Arias for Flute and Piano — B577 - HL240978
Arias for Flute Choir — B583 - HL240979
Arias for Two Flutes and Piano — B584 - HL240981

SOLOS (with piano accompaniment unless otherwise stated)

Giulio Briccialdi, arr. Sir James Galway
The Carnival of Venice (Il Carnevale di Venezia) — SU797 - HL240977
Eugene Magalif
For Tanya (opt. Flute 2 and Wind Chimes) — SU810 - HL244914
Eugene Magalif
Romance — SU811 - HL244916
Eugene Magalif
Revelation — SU809 - HL244915
Jules Mouquet, ed. Sir James Galway
La Flute de Pan — SU804 - HL240982
Johann Quantz, ed. Sir James Galway
Concerto in G Major — SU805 - HL240983
M.A. Reichert, arr. Sir James Galway
The Encore Solo (unaccompanied) — SU794 - HL240984
Paul Taffanel, ed. Sir James Galway
Grand Fantasy on Mignon — SU795 - HL240985
Paul Wetzger, arr. Sir James Galway
Am Waldesbach (By the Forest Brook), Op. 33 — SU798 - HL240986
Charles-Marie Widor, ed. Sir James Galway
Suite — SU803 - HL240987

Southern MUSIC
EXCLUSIVELY DISTRIBUTED BY
Hal•Leonard®

keisersouthernmusic.com
Questions/ comments? info@southernmusic.com

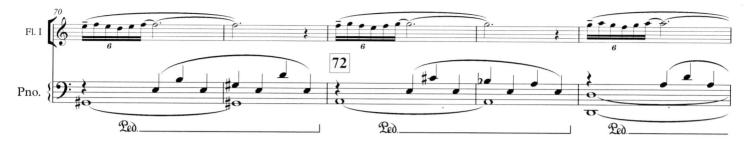

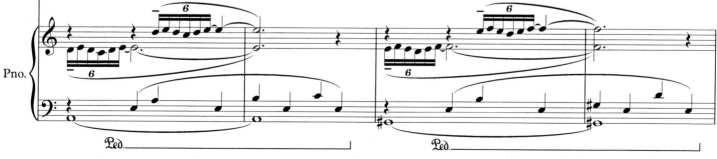

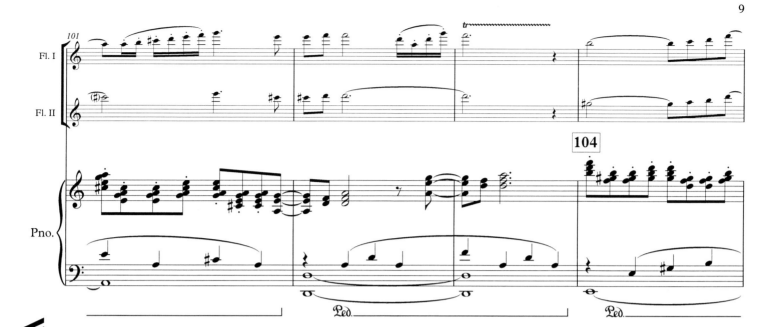

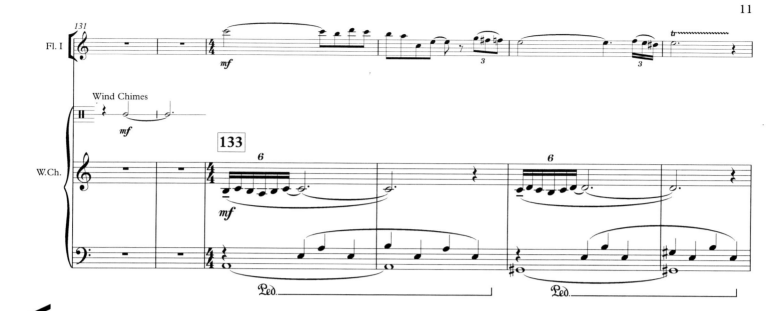

12

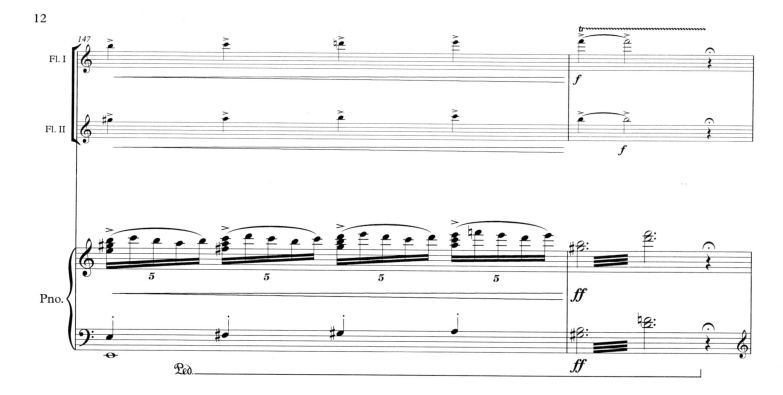

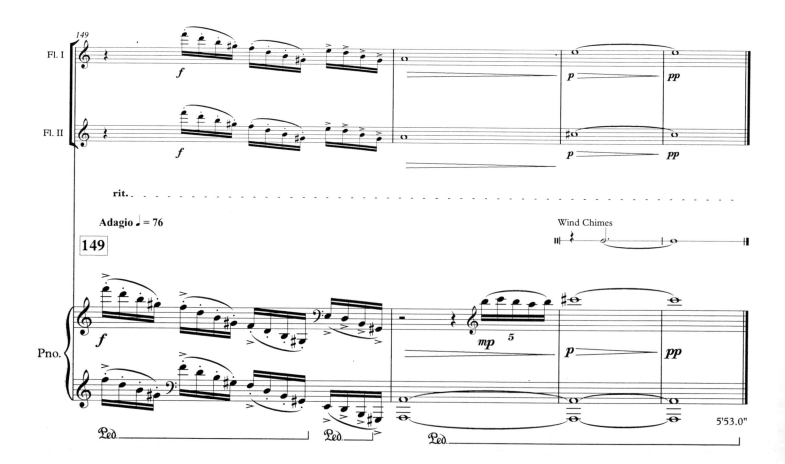

Flute II

For my lovely wife
For TANYA

Eugene Magalif, ASCAP

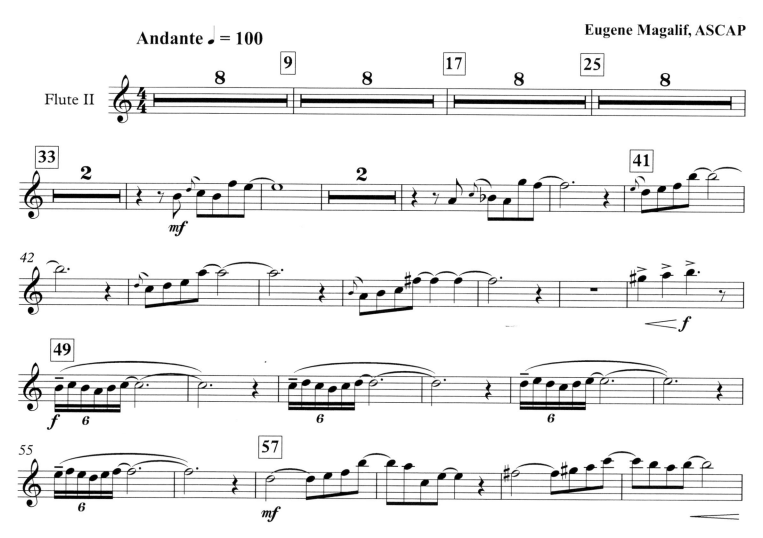

Eugene MAGALIF

For Tanya
for Flute and Piano
(with optional Flute 2 and Wind Chimes)

For my lovely wife